YOU WILL THRIVE

The Life-Affirming Way to Work and Become What You Really Desire

Jag Shoker

BENNION
KEARNY

To all my friends.
Chase your real dream in life.
Have faith that you will thrive.

About the Author

Jag Shoker is a leading performance coach working with high profile and talented individuals in business, sport, and entertainment. He is the author of 'The 7 Master Moves of Success' and 'Playing the Beautiful Game' and is also an engaging and dynamic motivational speaker who works with a diverse range of audiences and leading organisations.

Whether it is through his books, his speaking, or his coaching work, Jag is deeply passionate about helping others to express their talent and fulfil their true potential.

Acknowledgements

This book is dedicated to:

All the great teachers who I have had the real privilege and good fortune of meeting on the Way. You have shown me the joy, wonder, and importance of becoming a student of life. This book is my humble attempt to share with others the great wisdom you have so freely given to me.

All my clients who have put their trust in me. This book reflects so many of the discoveries we have made in our sessions. You will no doubt recognise the life-affirming journey that it reveals; for each and every one of you has made the courageous decision to follow your heart and go all the Way in becoming what you really desire.

All my family. I am forever grateful for your loving support. You uplift my Work and you inspire my Way.

Finally, a special thank you to James Lumsden-Cook from Bennion Kearny. Thank you for believing in my Work and for publishing this book. It is much appreciated.

Table of Contents

Introduction   1

1: Seek the Way ahead that matters   7

2: Do what you love to open up the Way   21

3: Keep the faith when life tests you   33

4: Now decide who you are going to be   49

5: Earn the right to get ahead   63

6: Master the Way to express yourself   81

Epilogue: Remember the Way   95

INTRODUCTION

Eight years ago, I was handed a newspaper article by a friend who I was meeting for coffee. It featured the story of a man who had started life as a taxi driver but who had – through a remarkable career – become the personal manager and close friend to one of the world's most recognised and influential sporting celebrities.

He then said something that surprised me.

"You need to meet this guy!" he told me excitedly.

"Why and how would we ever meet?" I replied.

"I don't know. I just get the feeling you need to meet this guy," he replied in all seriousness.

Without giving it too much thought, I moved the conversation on. The idea seemed a little farfetched. At the time the man in question lived in another country and worked in another world entirely different to the conventional world of banking in which I found myself at the time. It seemed crazy to entertain any notion that the two of us would ever meet. But here's the craziest part of it all, four years later we did meet and over time it became increasingly apparent that we needed to meet.

So what brought us together?

I will reveal the remarkable sequence of events later in the book. However, this book is not about my story. Nor that of the man in the article, for that is his terrific story to tell. It is about the *life-affirming path* that unfolds when you make the *definite* decision to follow your heart; the decision to pursue the work in life that will allow you to thrive and become whom you really desire to be. *That process is revealed in every page of this book.*

In writing this book, I hope to bring the magic of life to your attention once more and to open your eyes to the uplifting possibility that some *great orchestrating power* is actively working from behind the scenes for yours and everybody else's highest good.

As you'll discover, when you pursue your most heartfelt dream in life and you have the courage to take the many big leaps of faith that this path demands, life becomes attuned to your heartfelt desire. *Signs* appear to point you in a certain direction and favourable situations – *frequently unforeseen and unexpected* – occur *just* when they are needed and often when you are hard pushed by a difficult set of circumstances that have besieged you. It is then that the right people and right opportunities converge on your path with such *timely precision* that it appears as if the *magic of life* has contrived a Way to make what you most desire, or desperately require, to happen.

As I'll share later, I do not use the term 'magic' lightly in this book. I use it to refer to the definite possibility that *there is a greater power that resides within you,* which is a tremendous force for good; and which can somehow transcend space and time and *attract* all you need to make your Way through life.

I believe it does not matter how you refer to this power. Whether you believe it is spiritual, mental, emotional, or physical in origin is immaterial. Whether you call it God, Providence, personal magnetism, or the power of attraction does not make a difference. What is important is that you consciously use this great power to transform yourself and the life you live.

I believe you can invoke this power when you follow your heart and pursue *the Way to get ahead* in life that matters the most to you. This is the path that is revealed by your heart that guides you to the career or calling through which *you will thrive. In time* – after much testing of your *belief* – it leads to the perfect stage in life that frees you to *express yourself and become everything you desire to be.*

This book points out *the Way* to boldly pursue that heartfelt dream and the *Work* that is required to make it happen. Know that the greater the dream the greater the Work required to manifest it.

But let me be clear about what actually constitutes the Work:

The Work is making the necessary effort to turn your inspiration into application.

Inspiration within this book comes from knowing who you most want to be and what you most want to do. It comes from *finding a greater purpose in life* that calls upon you to *give your best* and make the most of your talent.

Application is doing the transformational Work that is required to make it all happen.

I am intimately acquainted with the Way and the Work required to get ahead. As I reveal later, it is the path I follow and the one that I help others to pursue to greater effect and with greater success.

As the author of this book, I humbly confess that I cannot say that this book *definitively* tells you the Way to succeed in life. I'm happy to concede that I do not possess the omniscience to claim that it is based on some infallible or absolute Universal laws that guarantee your success!

However, it has been said that 'once is chance, twice is coincidence and three times or more is a pattern'. In helping others to find the Way to get ahead, I have *repeatedly* seen certain patterns play out time and time again. This book points out those patterns. I believe you will see them when you give everything you have to pursue the great dream that is lodged securely in your heart.

Much of what is written in this short guide distils the essence of what I wrote about in my previous book *The 7 Master Moves of Success*. That book shares a scientific and a common sense approach to creating success that few would refute but not many are prepared to apply.

At times, however, this book may stretch your imagination and belief. I may, on occasion, use words or language that require *faith* on your part if you are to act on them.

In writing this book, it is not my intention to convince you that you should simply believe what I believe. I can say that every word and sentence it contains is offered to you the reader because my head, heart, and intuition lead me to believe that they are true and beneficial. However, I would simply urge you to keep an open mind to what you read. Treat this book as a *working hypothesis*, on what to expect when you follow your heart to become that something more you desire. As such, test what is written against your own intuition and experience. As I suggest later, get your heart in the right place and see what transpires!

My humble hope is that this book will be a motivational call to action. May it inspire you to find the perfect opportunity to *express yourself and give your best to a worthy cause.* It is worth re-reading these last words in italics. They are key to what this whole book is about. They reveal the very essence of *the Way to thrive* in life.

In pursuing the Way, you will discover latent talents and abilities that the world needs and that life will call upon you to give unreservedly. In *giving* your best, I am convinced you will find the greater sense of fulfilment that may have eluded you up until now.

It is important to know that the Way to get ahead is not a selfish or blind pursuit of personal ambition. It is much more noble and uplifting than that. But know that great demands will be made upon you – if what you *desire* in your heart is to become something real that you can see, feel, and taste.

When you step foot on the Way, it will become clear that life will test you but also that Providence will guide you. Always remember that if you ever lose your Way, do not lose your heart. Nothing but good will flow from your decision to persevere with the Way and to stick with the Work.

The further ahead you go, the greater the rewards will flow. The more you do the Work, the greater the power you'll unleash within to effortlessly, fearlessly, and masterfully give your best – especially in the significant moments in your life when it is very much called for and needed.

The Way begins now by finding the inspiration you seek.

CHAPTER 1

Seek the Way ahead that matters

You may be reading these words because you are seeking a better way to go in life. You may be looking for that heartfelt motivation – *that inner spark* – which can help you to know exactly who you want to be, and exactly what you want to do.

Like many, you may have lost your way, lost your passion, or lost your motivation. Like many, you may be struggling to articulate any compelling sense of purpose in life. And herein lies the problem. If you do not know your purpose, how can you find the Way to get ahead in life and thrive doing what you really desire?

Like many, you may be caught up in a race – *a frantic race to get ahead.* This race, which can dominate much of how we think, feel, and act, is the desire to climb the ladder of success. It is the race to gain more status and influence. It is the race to get ahead of *others.*

To win the race, you must either *have the best* or *be the best.*

There is nothing inherently wrong with either of these desires when they are pursued honestly and earnestly. If you are driven by the desire to have the best – the best clothes, the best car, the best house, the best possessions that you can afford – this is a good motivation. Many people around the world work hard to experience the pleasure and excitement of having something better. Much by way of wealth, employment, and opportunity is created by this material desire.

If the desire to have the best arouses the desire in you to *be* the best, it will inspire you to compete with the best, to reach new heights and to push your talent to a level that you may never have experienced without the driving force of this ambition.

The problems come when the race to get ahead is pursued as an end in itself, or as if it is the only purpose in life. When competition to have the best or be the best becomes all-consuming it can bring out the very worst in us. As the good and bad forces at work in the world remind us, man has both a higher and lower nature. As has been said before, man can rise higher than an angel or sink lower than a beast. Unfortunately, when the good and honest aspiration to get ahead stirs up man's lower nature, the race to get ahead descends into what has unceremoniously been called the *rat race.*

The rat race can reduce life to nothing but a zero-sum game – for every winner, there must be a loser; for someone to feel good, somebody must feel bad; for somebody to come out on top, somebody must prop up the pack from below.

The taxing and relentless nature of the rat race causes many to seek expedient shortcuts to get ahead for the race mercilessly stops for no-one.

Instead of earning the right to have the best or be the best, some turn instead to giving off the *impression* that they are doing well by buying conspicuous expensive purchases; even if that means getting stuck in a well-paid profession or getting shackled with a level of debt that kills their spirit and sense of adventure.

The rat race also takes a nasty turn for the worse when man is willing to cheat the system by stepping on others or by holding others back. The noble ladder of success is then replaced by the "greasy pole" to the top as blind personal ambition is pursued with no consideration of the collateral damage it causes. People in positions of responsibility who are meant to serve our best interests 'sell out' and gratuitously serve their own interests. They abuse their positions to get ahead and stay ahead by denying others their fair share of opportunity. It is the use of these Machiavellian tactics that perhaps gives the rat race its lowly reputation. As it has been suggested, if you do win the rat race, by definition you're still a rat!

Keep your feet firmly planted on the noble ladder of success. Cheating the system is not the Way.

When the race to get ahead does bring out the worst in us there is a real danger that it can leave much destruction in its wake. There is natural anger if you are denied the opportunity to get ahead or if you feel like you have been cast aside and cut adrift from those in the leading pack.

The inability of so many to get a foothold in the race to get ahead divides many nations, organisations, and communities. There is a real tangible threat to the 'good life' that so many of us are striving to achieve as ever larger numbers of people feel disenchanted and disenfranchised with the way things are.

The race for wealth and status is also responsible for much illness and anxiety as people seek to get ahead at *all* costs. The Dalai Lama poignantly summed up the plight of man, when he was asked what surprised him most about humanity:

"Man," he replied, "because he sacrifices his health in order to make money. Then he sacrifices money to recuperate his health. And then he is so anxious about the future that he does not enjoy the present; the result being that he does not live in the present or the future; he lives as if he is never going to die, and then dies having never really lived."

The disillusionment with the rat race is creating a wide feeling of angst; many people now share the same fear of being *found out*. Outwardly, they give the impression that they are thriving in the face of fierce competition, that they have what it takes to survive in a 'dog eat dog' world. They give the impression that they are good, tough, and strong enough to mix it with whomever, whenever, and however.

Inwardly, however, many feel tired, exhausted, and anxious. Many feel that they are not as good as they outwardly portray themselves to be. Many feel that they can't keep up or cope with the demands that are being placed upon them. Many feel uninspired. Many feel unwell. Many feel that they are just going through the motions as their heart is not in their work.

Are you like so many people who think, "What's the point to it all? Is the stress of getting ahead in life really worth it?"

If the race to get ahead of others is beginning to make you feel tired, ill, and disheartened it may be time for you to seek out a better Way to go in life. If you feel like you have lost your spark and lost your Way, it may be the time to seek something *more* in life – *something greater that will inspire your mind and appeal to your heart.*

Find meaning in what you do and you'll spark the Way into life.

Many people are now discovering a growing urge within themselves to find a Way of living and succeeding that has more *meaning*. More and more people are seeking a better and more fulfilling Way of life. Many of us want to do something with *greater purpose*, something that can carry us beyond the narrow and selfish confines of our personal ambitions; something that *matters* in the world.

I believe this change in direction is being inspired by a collective awakening of the intelligence that resides in our hearts. As we increasingly feel the desire to follow our hearts, we are seeking out work that involves doing something we deeply *care* about. As this awakening gathers pace, I believe more and more people will turn their thoughts from having the best and being the best to the rewarding purpose of *giving their best.*

Organisations, large and small, are now picking up on this sea change. They are under pressure to show their people that what they do makes a positive contribution to life and serves a *greater purpose* beyond self-interest, earning profit, or edging in front of the competition in a neverending cycle of attack and counter-attack.

This growing desire to Work for some greater purpose is why some of the most forward-thinking and talented individuals amongst us are prepared, if necessary, to take a risk and go it alone in a bid to make a greater difference.

**To thrive turn your thoughts from having
the best or being the best to the uplifting
Work of giving your best.**

Like many other who are now following their hearts, you too may be seeking this *greater purpose* that *calls* for you to *give* your best.

This is the Way to thrive, and this is where the search for it really begins.

If you listen carefully enough, you will hear a voice deep within you which is urging you to find your *calling.* This is the Way to get ahead that stirs your heart into action. It is the Work that gives you the perfect platform to use your talent to meet some definite need in the world.

To find your calling, you must look for what inspires you to make a difference in life. This inspiration will unlock within you the power and desire to do the Work that life *demands* if you are to turn your heartfelt dream into a glorious reality.

This Work is the ability to turn your inspiration into application.

When you commit to the Work, you will discover an ability to *attract* the opportunities, people, and situations that you need to get ahead – not ahead *of* others but ahead *with* others. This is the real difference of following your heart to get ahead; getting ahead is no longer *just* about having the best or being

13

the best yourself. The Way to get ahead that appeals to your heart will *inspire* you to connect with others who share your inspiration and build with those who share your purpose. I believe this is why the Way to get ahead will take you further in life – as one African proverb states, "If you want to go quickly go alone. If you want to go far, go together."

Life is more than a zero sum game.
Your heart wants to do something that adds
to the world.

But how can you find the Way to get ahead that appeals the most to your heart? How will you know what your calling is? Where will you find your spark of inspiration that empowers you to thrive?

Finding answers to these questions can be frustrating. It can be vexing to know that you want something better in life, but you just don't know *what*. But it doesn't need to be that way.

I firmly believe that if you listen to your heart, your *intuition* will speak to you. It *knows* the Way to get ahead. It can give you all the answers you need.

To follow your heart, you must trust your intuition.

But first, you will need to learn how to listen to its voice. That voice will speak to you as a clear thought or feeling which leads you in a *definite* direction. If you let it guide you, you will see it always shows you how to get ahead in the best possible Way.

However, it is not always easy to tune into your intuition. It will not typically assert itself over your mind which often noisily churns away with a neverending stream of thoughts. You must become *still* and *calm* to hear its voice. If you can relax your body and quieten your mind, you will discover that it will give you firm conviction of what you need to do and the Way you need to go.

I have come to appreciate that my intuition will always guide my Way and put me in touch with my *highest good*. Somehow it appears to be able to reach out into my desired future and then point to what direction I must take today. When it guides me, I *know* that in that moment whatever it suggests is the right thing, the right solution, or the right idea that meets my immediate need. I may not initially be able to reason out its guidance fully, but I have repeatedly found that the reason always becomes evident at some later or relevant point on the Way.

Your heart knows the Way to get ahead.

Listen with a quiet mind and it will reveal

the Way to go.

However, know that your intuition is not an impulsive voice that urges you to do something whimsical or reckless in life. It will have been with you for a long time in the background of your mind and the innermost chamber of your heart, waiting patiently for you to recognise it.

Know that it is not a voice that will tell you to do (or be) something selfish. If you follow your heart and trust your intuition, it will always lead you to the greatest possible good for all concerned in each and every situation you face.

It is this opportunity to do good and to be great that appeals to your heart.

Be open to how your intuition may inspire you to seek out this opportunity in life. It may speak to you through a recurring dream in which you are doing and being something more inspiring. It may speak to you when you are most disheartened with the way things are, and you are most in need of some *divine intervention*. It may, when you least expect it, and often when you most need it, provide you with a spark that comes disguised in many forms; you may run into someone who is a blast from the past; you may rediscover a book that once uplifted you; you may listen to a song that once moved you; or you may see a film again that once excited you.

It is highly likely that your intuition may take you back to a time – like your childhood or early adult years – when you imagined more exciting possibilities; ones that you may have forgotten about in the mad desire to get ahead of others.

If you can reconnect with the people, the books, the music, the films, the thoughts, and the feelings that once made your heart sing, a flood of forgotten memories, hopes and aspirations *will* come back to you. As they do, you may begin to rediscover the heartfelt dreams that you once entertained; dreams that have the power to stir your tired or sleepy heart back into life again if your motivation is lacking.

> The inspiration you need may come disguised in many forms. Be open to how your heart reveals the Way.

You may be asking 'what is intuition'? Is it a profound intelligence in your heart? Is it the voice of your soul? Is it a super-conscious state of mind? Is it a 'higher' intelligence in your brain?

This is something I believe we must each discover for ourselves. By definition, the answer lies *within* us. *Intuition is tuition from within.* It is in keeping with the original meaning of the word 'education' which means to *"bring or draw out".*

I believe that finding the source of your intuition is one of life's spiritual quests. Through it, we come to *know, trust,* and *rely* on a power greater than ourselves. It is this *inner power* that we start to consciously express outwards when we become aware of the Way to get ahead that appeals to the heart and makes the best use of our talent.

What we label that power is secondary. Appreciating it and putting it to *good* use in life is of vital concern for there is a great need in the world at this time for all of us to find better ways to be, regardless of what it is that we do.

For life is more than just a material pursuit. It is more than just a race to have more than your fellow man. It is an opportunity to learn, to grow, to imagine, and to create, for the good of all concerned.

If you don't know your calling yet, trust in your heart and intuition; they will reveal the Way to go. They will give you *the courage to dream* of a better future.

That may sound like a strange statement to you. *Does it take courage to simply dream?*

In my experience it does. Many people are reluctant to dream of greater possibilities that may seem beyond their reach. They call themselves 'realists' but often their unwillingness to dream is a defence mechanism that saves them from the pain and disappointment that false hope or failed aspiration brings. Others do the reverse; they fancifully dream too much. They harbour extravagant pipedreams that they know they will never act upon, thus saving themselves from the very same disappointment that the 'realistic non-dreamer' wishes to avoid. To dream of a greater possibility – which today appears beyond your reach – takes courage. To act upon that dream takes greater courage still. If you can discover what your inspiration – your heartfelt dream – actually is, it will bring with it all the courage you need to make it a reality.

You already have all the courage you need. Dream of bolder possibilities that stir your heart into action.

Do not lose heart if you do not, at this stage, know what that heartfelt dream is. Do not lose heart if you cannot see the Way to get ahead that matters most to you. Have *faith* that your intuition will show you the Way. It will give the *inspirational idea* you need to spark your dream into life. It is likely you will only dimly sense this idea at first. You may only vaguely see that the Way you will thrive lies in a certain direction. However, if you can follow your heart and pursue your passion, you will see that the Way to get ahead will unfold from right where you are.

The Work – as ever – will be to follow the Way as far as you can go.

CHAPTER 2

Do what you love to open up the Way

Inspiration is a wonderful thing. It lifts you into a higher dimension of thought and feeling. When you are inspired by the Way ahead, you feel unconstrained by limitations and anything seems possible. The vision of what 'might be' captivates you and urges you to take action. Your heart begins to call out to you. If you could hear it speak, it would most probably say:

'Do not let life pass you by. Make the most of your talent. Give everything you have to something you believe in.'

The time is now to turn your inspiration into application. The Work begins here.

But before you take your first meaningful step on the Way, *pause for a moment.* Reflect back on any success you may have achieved when your principle desire was to have the best or be the best. No doubt the rewards of success *felt good.* Having the best felt good. Being the best felt good. Rising up the ladder of success felt good. Being recognised for your talent felt good.

It goes without saying that on a *personal* level, success is deeply gratifying; so why point out the obvious? There is a good reason. When we start thinking about doing what *matters* most to us, and how we can use our gifts to give something back to life, we can fall into the trap of becoming morbidly serious.

It is true that when you sense the Way, and see a greater purpose to life, it calls on you to give more when and where it is needed. It becomes clear that others are relying on you. There is, therefore, most definitely a *need* for you to perform. You know that by stepping up your game you can make a tangible difference to the lives of others; and you know that the more talent you possess the more others will expect and demand from you.

This need to give your best can feel like a weighty responsibility and become a heavy burden to bear. However, if your calling feel likes like an *obligation* to you, I would say stop right where you are! This is not how following your heart should feel and it is unlikely to result in you giving your best. Ask yourself this: whenever you have done something through obligation, has it ever brought the best out of you? I would hazard a guess that the answer in most cases is no.

Do not mistake this as the Way. Too many people, with honourable intentions, do what they feel they *should* do or *ought* to do, but not what it is in their hearts that they really *want* to. That, in my experience, is not an inspired way to live. It rarely leads to the fulfilment you desire.

There is no obligation when pursuing the Way. Simply follow your heart and do what feels good.

Know that the Way to get ahead is not one of forced obligation that wears you down and kills your spirit. That path will lead to much resentment and bitterness if you wake up one day and feel as though you have given too much of yourself into the bargain. If doing your Work turns into a thankless or joyless task there is a great risk you will lose your Way and be led astray by many competing passions and temptations.

The Way to get ahead is an opportunity to thrive by living a fuller and more meaningful life. It is the chance to serve some great purpose that adds to the world. What that purpose is, is something that *you* must decide for yourself. Only you can know the direction to take in life that will most excite your heart.

The great opportunity before you now is to find the best Way to use your talent to do something you care about; to do something rewarding; to do something that you *love*.

Know that it is love that always turns your inspiration into application. When inspired by a great love of what we do, each and everyone one of us (regardless of our profession or calling) *gives our best without reservation.* Artists shape things of beauty, writers pen words of inspiration, actors reach the height of self-expression, athletes defy limitations, leaders embody greatness, and teachers inspire others to strive for greatness. There is not a man or woman alive whose Work is not transformed by the love of what they do.

> **Pursue your passion! Do what you love and nothing will hold you back from giving your best.**

If you commit to the Work of pursuing your passion, and doing what you love, your passion will carry you to ever-increasing heights. You will not hold back from giving your best. Your calling will spur you on to know more, experience more, do more, and be more. Your passion for what you do will drive you to present your unique gift to the world in the best possible Way. It is the passion for the Work that compels you to always break new ground and make the most of your talent.

When your passion compels you to contribute everything you have to what matters most to you, it then becomes your *ruling passion.* All other 'lesser' and competing interests fall away. Your life will then take on a new degree of clarity as this one ruling passion takes centre stage and releases the power within you – the WILL – to perfect your skill and to master your craft.

When you pursue your passion, not only will you strive for something bigger and better but also for something *beautiful and beneficial.* At the height of your self-expression, everything you do becomes a work of art. It is here that we now pick up the Work. To go forward with your passion you must first *go within.* The Work, now, is to go into your imagination and *get an idea of what you would most love to do in life.*

This idea will then become the *ideal* that you want to pursue, the dream you want to chase, and the vision you want to make real. In time, it will reveal the Way to get ahead.

Imagine this desired vision of your future as often as you can. Dream of what may become. Let it be the inspiration that wakes you each morning. Let it be the final thought that sends you to sleep each night.

To imagine the exciting possibilities that lie ahead of you, you may need to train your imagination. Some of you will have to unlock your power to imagine. Others will need to learn to channel it in a positive direction. Some of you will need to hold it back from running riot in your mind with a 1,001 competing thoughts and desires.

The best way to train your imagination is to always imagine what you would love to see happen in your future. See it as best you can. *Love* what you are doing. *Love* how good you feel. *Love* the difference you are making by fully expressing your talent. *Love* this dream as though it was all unfolding right now in your life.

This love you feel then becomes a force of nature. It connects you directly with that incredibly creative, resourceful, and relentless force within you that is your willpower. This *will* is an *intrinsic* form of desire. When we desire to have the best or be the best, we are attracted by the desirable things we see *outside* ourselves. When we are motivated by pursuing the Way – that inspirational idea of what we would most love to do – our heart desires nothing more than to manifest this dream we see *within* us. Know that love (when recognised as a force of nature) is not just some sentimental notion. *Love is the power of attraction*. By some powerful and invisible means it seems to attract everything it needs to create what it desires. Time and time again I have seen that it has the power to *orchestrate* events and create all the right circumstances you need to succeed in life. When you pursue your passion, a consistent *pattern* seems to play out; *life contrives a way to make it happen.* When you imagine receiving all the good things your heart desires, 'Providence', or the guiding hand of fate, appears to provide some form of material assistance to help make it happen.

When you do what you love, you will open up the Way.

Life becomes attuned to your heartfelt desire. Meaningful coincidences take place, *signs* appear to point you in a certain direction and favourable situations – *frequently unforeseen and unexpected* – present themselves *just* when they are needed. The right people, the right circumstances and right opportunities converge on your path with such *timely precision* that it appears as if the world has listened in to your heartfelt desires and responded in kind by opening up the Way.

I know full well that you will have to take the last three paragraphs on *faith*. It is not easy to believe in Providence or some kind of higher or protective power. It's not always easy, with all the troubles we see in the world, to believe that we live in a kind and beneficent Universe that works for our highest good.

Love is a force of nature.
It will attract everything you need
to thrive in what you do.

However, if Providence, God, or some higher spiritual energy does exist, I believe (as I have experienced) that the goodness of your desires wins its backing. I firmly believe all good desires will be fulfilled in time. In my humble opinion, life works for you when you are prepared to work for life. Life will serve you when you are ready to serve life and enter into the great spirit of giving and receiving.

Naturally, I do not expect you to simply believe what I believe or accept my truth as your own truth. I would, however, urge you to put it to the test. Treat this whole book as the *working hypothesis* it is intended to be. *Imagine* if the points in this book that require your faith – those that are currently beyond scientific proof – are true. *Act* as if they are true and judge them by your own results and experiences. Get your heart in the right place and see what transpires. Seek the Way to get ahead that your heart truly desires and watch with interest where it takes you.

Without doubt when you *live your passion* and love what you do, you will experience a definite feeling of being *magnetic;* that you can draw towards you all that you need. As such, the Way will always unfold from where you are. You will discover that you are always right where you need to be even though you may not be able to see it at the time in question.

As your passion for your dream grows, your power to attract the right opportunities increases, and your Way becomes more evident, the time will surely come when you are ready to take the Work to another level. You will need to *take a leap of faith and commit to your dream* if you are to continue to follow your heart to where it wishes to lead you.

You will know when the time has come for you to take that leap, for your heart will ask you to take a *risk* and step out into an unknown and uncertain future to do the Work that you love.

> **The Way always unfolds from right**
> **where you are. Look for signs**
> **that point the Way to go.**

Only the most courageous and passionate of people grasp this moment of destiny with both hands. Only those who truly trust in their heart and intuition take this leap of faith.

Know that every leap of faith on the Way (and there will be many) is a decision you must make *wholeheartedly*. Few of us are every really prepared to do this. As the author Ordway Tead pointed out in his book *The Art of Leadership* (1929), "So many people are loath to make irrevocable decisions, are tepid in their enthusiasms, timid in their faith in themselves and others, afraid of the burden of responsibility and undecided about their direction."

If you are now facing your first big leap of faith, it is vital that you remain open to your intuition. Something will nudge you forward and give you the belief that everything will work out if you have the courage to take this leap. This nudge may come in many different guises. As one esoteric saying hints at, "Angels often speak to us through the nearest available voice." It might be a book you read, a film you watch, or something that someone says to you that suddenly tips the balance in a positive direction and fills you full of hope that *you will succeed in realising your dream* if you commit to it with all your heart.

When you are genuinely ready to take your leap of faith, your fears will subside and this significant step forward in your life will feel exhilarating. The love of what you do at this stage outweighs any fears that hold you back, and you're able to *take the chance* that most definitely sends you on your Way.

This leap of faith is a momentous decision. It ripples out into the future and changes the course of your destiny. It paves the Way for all the good you desire to flow to you. It is highly likely that after taking your first leap of faith, you will experience what many bold adventurers – the followers of the Way – have referred to as *beginner's luck*. The chance you take pays off. You are able to capitalise on the immediate opportunity before you and you experience your first taste of success in the form of some *small but significant win* that takes you further.

This small win, this most necessary slice of beginner's luck, is reward for your courage. It is also a form of much needed encouragement for you to now push ahead with your dreams in the real hope that *you will make it*, that you can do it, and that you will achieve it. The belief gained from this win is priceless. It lights a spark of enthusiasm within you that cannot be extinguished. It frees your mind to entertain greater possibilities. It makes you feel that you can succeed more than you have ever done in the past. It encourages you to dream big and gives you every incentive to go further.

There will be many leaps of faith on the Way. Take a chance when your heart urges you to step out into the unknown.

This first success on the Way also starts the Work of *building faith*. Faith by its very nature is subjective. It is something you must discover within yourself. No-one can simply give you the deep faith that you will need on the Way. You will need to earn it with every hard fought victory and every bit of success that is achieved through overcoming failure.

The faith that you build will prove decisive; for now, expect that life will test how sincerely you believe in your heart. The Way to get ahead may not be easy. Following your heart may lead you directly into the eye of a storm. You will need to have faith if you are to make it through with your dream still intact.

CHAPTER 3

Keep the faith when life tests you

If you have acted on the vision in your heart and have experienced your own slice of beginner's luck, the Way before you could now take one of two different paths. Firstly, you may blaze an initial trail of glory, and experience a rapid rise to fame as you shine brightly doing what it is that you love. If your life proceeds down this fast moving path, the world will suddenly sit up and take notice of your exploits. People will start to take an interest in your Work. As your talents get recognised, you may become lauded as a potential riser to the top. As success flows thick and fast, you will most definitely feel like a man or woman on the up!

Alternatively, your initial success may be less eye-catching. As you pursue your passion, your progress may be slow and steady, but you will feel a positive difference through doing what you love.

Whether you explode out of the blocks, or your steps forward are more modest, your *belief* in what you do will grow. This enhanced belief feels very tangible. It courses through your veins. You feel more capable and free than normal. You feel more alive than ever. Physically, emotionally, and mentally you have more edge. Spiritually – if you are open to it – you may sense a greater power stirring within you.

Others too will feel your belief as it radiates outwards and makes you more magnetic and influential. With a growing ability to inspire others, you will really start to believe that you can change the world.

Driven on by your calling, your passion, and the love of what you do, you are likely to take more risks with every hope that they will come off. Having witnessed your power to attract the right opportunities your Way, you will go forward in life with a newfound confidence.

Your boldness can propel you into an exciting new realm of possibilities. The conventional or old way of doing things may no longer appeal to you. Riding high on belief, you will want to try new things. You will be prepared to go where you need to go. You will want to take chances and do what it takes to make progress. Driven on by an overriding belief in what you do, *everything will feel like it is meant to be.*

When realise your power to attract
everything you need, you will boldly go
where your heart leads you.

As your journey gathers pace, expect life's cynics and sceptics to have something to say about the daring new direction in life you are pursuing.

For those who prefer the safety, comfort, and predictability of the herd, your decision to break free and do something different will be disconcerting.

For those who prefer to 'keep up with the Joneses,' the desire to serve some greater calling will be perplexing.

For those who have never had the courage to dream, your decision to chase yours may be vexing.

For those engaged in the selfish pursuit of their personal ambitions, your desire to make a difference may prove nauseating.

For those who have a vested interest in keeping you where you are, your decision to go your own Way may even prove threatening.

No matter what the reason, know that your decision to follow your heart and pursue a better Way will always be challenged by those who prefer to keep things the way they are.

To keep you in your place they may tell you are too idealistic, that you dream too much, that you expect too much from life, that you are brave but foolish. They may tell you that what you wish for is never going to happen, that you have ideas above your station, or that you are naive to believe that *you* can change the world doing what you do.

Be prepared. At some point on the Way, you will face an onslaught of negative voices and opinions. If you allow them to get into your mind, you may start to doubt your own heart and question the Way ahead. If these doubts are allowed to grow in power, they will stir up within you two deeply human fears: *the fear of failure* and *the fear of public opinion*.

If your fears temporarily overpower the love of what you do, your thoughts will subtly shift from success to failure, from thriving to surviving, and from an overriding feeling of belief to that of doubt.

Everything changes when this happens. The vision within you loses its lustre. The desired Way ahead grows more difficult. And the dream you have pursued so passionately now seems less attainable.

If doubt is allowed to undermine what you do, you may start to hesitate and waver. You may start to question your ability. You may start to second guess every move you make. If you doubt you have the talent to pull it all off, your actions will lose the decisiveness they need to be effective. There is a real danger, then, that your ability to give your best may become compromised. Instead of focusing on the love of what you do, the fear of failure may start to dominate your thinking.

Negative voices will always question your Way. Do not let the fear of failure overpower the love for what you do.

Like so many who are unfortunate to lose their Way, you may discover that you have drastically fallen short of where you need to be.

It is at this point – as the Way ahead narrows and closes in – that everything else that can go wrong often *does* go wrong, and you find yourself caught up in a *crisis* when you least need it.

If you are now face to face with a crisis, you will see that (one by one) events can turn against you – often in both your professional *and* personal lives. If Providence contrived a way to help you in the past, it now seems to have taken wings; life appears to conspire *against* you.

Having taken a leap of faith to follow your heart, you can now find yourself alone in the wilderness. There is no longer a strong feeling of motivation, magnetism, or influence; there is simply a feeling of being cut off from your inspiration.

When such a crisis befalls you, *be prepared* for it to shake your foundations. Every ounce of belief you have built up along the Way will be severely tested, as will your desire to continue to follow your heart.

With every negative blow that lands during this crisis, life asks *how much do you really trust your heart?* As fear bangs loudly on your door, life asks *do you really believe in your dream?* And as the pain and disappointment of failure becomes more acute, life asks *why are you prepared to suffer so much for it?*

It is at this point that the *strength of your motivation* is questioned. Do you have the heart to go on or is fear going to stop you from doing what you love?

It is at this moment that the *sincerity* of your motive gets well and truly tested. Are you really looking to make a greater difference in life or is your dream really only about you?

Make no mistake about it; this is a most testing time. As your doubts and fears threaten to wrestle your dream away from you, life will test your resolve. As you rapidly approach the nadir of your crisis, you may be presented with an easy way out. Perhaps an old job comes calling, or a seemingly more glamorous path opens up, or perhaps you simply find a convenient reason to call time on your dream.

If the Way ahead of you is now massively uncertain, the Work you are required to do is clear enough if you do not want to relinquish the dream that matters most to you; you must decide what happens next.

With everything going against you, will you go on… or give in?

Many do now give in. Uncertain about the future and anxious about what lies ahead, they become consumed by incessant worries that things will turn out for the worst. They quit the Way that once appealed to their hearts and they take the 'easy' way out.

Know that when you face the worst of any crisis, the decision to go on and to remain standing will be a deeply visceral one for you may be deeply unsure of where to go and what to do next.

Be prepared for every ounce of your belief to be severely tested on the Way.

If your journey is not to end, and you are not to lose faith in your heart, *be prepared* that the crisis you face might get worse before it gets better. Every subsequent thing that may go wrong from this point onwards will be a *gut-wrenching test of your faith*. Only a strong heart can give you the stomach you need to make it through.

Know that a complete loss of faith at this or at any other stage along the Way can prove disastrous, for you may find yourself free falling into a very dark place, as this one story reveals:

There was a young man who ever since he could remember had absolute faith in life and in God. Deep down he knew his calling; he knew how he would thrive in life. He needed to use his faith and belief to follow his heart so that he could in time inspire others to do the same.

Then one day somebody asked him a question that made him doubt life.

"If there is a God and that God is good, why is there so much evil in the world?" he was asked.

He had no reply for he had never really contemplated evil. He had always aspired to be good. The young man became deeply unsettled by the question. He began to innocently contemplate why evil things happened in life but in doing so something terrible happened; the young man lost sight of himself in the process. As he did, his mind began to run riot with dark thoughts which made him doubt his own goodness.

As the young man lost his faith in life, he began to believe that deep down he might be bad and not good. As evil voices raged in his head and urged him to do hurtful things, he tried his best to force them out of his mind.

Unfortunately, the dark thoughts within him only grew louder and more powerful. Unable to remove them from his mind, the young man decided he didn't want to live anymore.

In every sleepless night that followed, he contemplated how to take his own life.

One night, in his darkest moment, as he battled hard against the evil voices within him, he instinctively cried out to God, "Help me! Help me!"

As he cried out in despair, he wondered why he had lost his mind, why he had lost his Way, and why the God he believed in since he was a young child had allowed it all to happen.

Just then he heard a Voice speak within him that cut through all the turmoil. He immediately recognised that it came from a good place.

"Why do you want to take your own life?" the Voice asked him lovingly.

"Because I don't want to hurt anyone," the young man cried back in anguish.

"So you would rather take your own life than hurt anyone else?"

"Yes," the young man replied.

"Well then you can't be bad," the Voice replied emphatically, "You must be good!"

That one thought saved the young man's life. It gave him belief in himself once more. One positive thought at a time, he rebuilt his mind, his life and his faith. Years later life when he had found his Way again he realised that the crisis he had faced had really been a test of character.

I know this story well for the young man facing the crisis was me. Having lost my faith in life, I ended up in a dark place that required me to use all my strength to get back out. I'm glad I did because I can now say to you, with firm conviction, that when you face your darkest hour, and there appears to be no Way forward, *find the faith to go on.*

When your heart is troubled by doubt, your mind is plagued by fear, and negativity submerges you in a terrible darkness, *hold onto the one positive thought you are able to believe in* and build your faith from there.

This one positive thought is like a glimmer of light. No matter how small, it is incredibly powerful for *light always has dominion over darkness.* Just as darkness must always give Way to light, I believe that positivity will always win out over negativity. However, there is one condition *you* must fulfil. The worrier in you that expects the worst must handover to the warrior within you who will fight for what is best.

In your darkest hour hold onto the one positive thought you can believe in. Your faith will grow from there.

This fight takes place on the inner battleground within your heart and mind where positive and negative thoughts wage war against each other. Your decision to commit to one side over the other swings the battle either way and shapes the story of how your life will play out. This battleground is symbolically portrayed in a Native American Cherokee story that will resonate with you deeply:

One evening an old Cherokee told his grandson about a battle that goes on inside people.

He said, "My son, the battle is between two wolves inside us all.

"One is Evil – It is anger, envy, jealousy, sorrow, regret, greed, arrogance, self-pity, guilt, resentment, inferiority, lies, false pride, superiority, and ego.

"The other is Good – It is joy, peace, love, hope, serenity, humility, kindness, benevolence, empathy, generosity, truth, compassion, and faith."

The grandson thought about it for a minute and then asked his grandfather: "Which wolf wins?"

The 'good wolf' – the warrior within you – is immensely powerful but you must allow it to fight the good fight. You must free it to fight for what you believe. You must trust it to help you go forward when fear threatens to hold you back.

The warrior within you can win the battle when you are facing your own personal crisis but you must remember one golden rule:

Think about the things you want to think about not the things you don't.

Re-read this last sentence many times. Let its implication and simplicity become clear to you. Your success will depend on it. Know that a strong mind is not built by trying to force negative thoughts out of your mind. As I learned the hard way, these thoughts will just grow in power and imprison you.

Instead, when your mind is plagued by doubts and fears, make an active effort to *substitute* negative thoughts that weaken you with those that are positive and uplift you. Know that if you can do this, you will always go far in life, for nothing can hold back a strong heart that believes in something good and a strong mind that is forever willing to Work towards it.

This, however, is easier said than done. It is easy to think positively when you're on the up, and everything is going your Way. It takes real heart and resilience to keep the faith when you are surrounded by the darkness and despair of a major crisis.

But you must keep the faith if your journey is to continue. You must find that one thought that will keep your hopes alive. I have discovered that there is one thought that allows most of us to cling to our faith in desperate times – it is that *everything happens for a reason*. It is clear that a crisis will *severely* test the very fabric of your character. Have faith, however, that this test is for a good reason. Have faith that at this critical point on the Way *life is not meant to break you but make you.*

Have faith that nature is infinitely wise in how she tests you. I believe that in any crisis, every man or woman is tested to the extent of his or her capabilities. Depending on where you are on your journey and on the strength of heart and mind you possess, these tests may be great or small, but they will always be significant.

Have faith when you get tested on the Way.
Remember life is not meant to break you
but make you.

Have faith that this gruelling test of character is needed to draw forth a latent quality within you that you will most definitely need along the Way. It is often when you have been made to *thrive under pressure* that you realise this quality. Have faith that you may not have discovered it had it not been for this crisis. As Winston Churchill once said, "Never let a good crisis go to waste." Have faith that any crisis you face gives you the best opportunity to build your strength and galvanise your character.

Have faith that you have, within you, a greater power to overcome all and any obstacles. Have faith that any crisis you face provides you with the perfect opportunity to demonstrate the strength of this power.

Have faith that just like before, when the right opportunities came your Way, you are still exactly where you need to be in life. This crisis you face is your opportunity to learn and grow. Have faith that *this crisis will pass* and that you will one day understand why it was so necessary, why it was so hard, and why the events in your life had to play out as they did.

Have faith, if your faith can stretch this far, that you live in a good and beneficent Universe. Have faith that there is a Higher Power at work that is wisely and surely building towards yours and everybody else's highest good, and that despite all that is presently wrong with the world this greater good will come to pass.

Have faith there is a Greater Plan of which you are a part and in which you must *play your part*; and that if your heart is in the right place everything will work out in time, regardless of how adverse your circumstances appear today.

Most importantly have faith in the goodness of your desires. Know why your dream matters. Imagine what the world would be denied if you didn't shine your light, if you didn't express your talent, and if you didn't give life your best.

Have faith that the full power, greatness, and goodness of life lies at your disposal if you seek to use this power in some uplifting Way that makes a positive difference in life. Know that if you can put your talent to good use, you will become a source of inspiration to others, and that they too may have the courage to follow their heart and pursue their dream.

Have faith in the goodness of your desires.
Believe everything will work out when your
heart is firmly in the right place.

If, at this time, you have found your calling in life but you have momentarily lost your Way, stay strong and resolute. Life needs you to keep the faith in your vision, your talent, and in your heartfelt dream. The world needs you to thrive and give your best more now than ever. Whether you are conscious of it or not, many people are deeply in need of the inspiration that only you can provide.

If life is testing you, have the courage to press on and persevere through the hard times. Keep the faith and know that the help you need is most assuredly on the Way. Providence is always ready to step back into the fray at just the right time when you call out for its inspiration.

CHAPTER 4

Now decide who you are going to be

There is a blessing in every situation, no matter how difficult circumstances may be. It may, however, take some time before the 'silver lining' of any crisis is revealed and for the Way ahead to become clear again.

Having made the courageous decision to go on with your dream despite the difficulties you face, there is still another element of the crisis that you must find the strength to bear; it is the feeling that you have been left on your own with nowhere to go and no-one (it seems) to turn to.

In this dreaded period of isolation, you cannot escape your thoughts. You cannot escape your circumstances. Most of all, you cannot escape yourself. At this time you will have to honestly ask yourself whether you possess the character that is needed to withstand the worst case scenario that may befall you.

You must have the courage to see yourself without any self-deception, self-delusion, or self-pity when your character is laid bare, and any false pretences you may have about yourself are exposed.

It is natural to feel discouraged when life reveals your weaknesses or shatters any false hopes you may have been harbouring, but take comfort from the fact that the Work needed to progress will become clear. You will know without a doubt what specific limitation you must overcome. You will know what definite changes you will need to make in order to transform yourself and to prevent your dream being discarded onto the scrap heap of unfulfilled hopes that may later come back to haunt you.

However, despite knowing what you need to do, you may not know *how* to go about it. As such you may feel like you are *helplessly* stuck in a rut that has trapped you and your aspirations. If you find yourself in such a predicament it will profit you greatly to remember something that I have come to rely on many times, and that is:

> *You are never on your own as you make your Way through life. The help you stand in need of will always be forthcoming when you ask for it. Providence always lies in wait ready to serve you just when you most need it.*

When you do *ask for help with all your heart*, I believe that some form of material assistance will come your Way to get you through the present crisis. We knowingly, or unknowingly, call forth this help when we hold our hands up in despair and literally look up to the heavens and say, *"Give me a break!"*

I believe, *without doubt,* that the break, opportunity, or assistance we need at this time, will *always* come when we play this 'help card'.

**Providence is always ready to step back into
the fray when you most need its inspiration.**

This card, however, must be played wisely. If you seek help too early in any period of difficulty, you may cheat yourself out of some much needed experience or personal growth; for you are always strengthened by any struggle in which you choose to remain strong in the face of adversity.

Alternatively, if you play your help card too late, perhaps believing that you are above the need for help, you may suffer greatly if arrogance or stubbornness takes hold of you which then brings you and your dreams crashing back down to earth.

If, however, you play the help card having earnestly given it your all in any situation, I believe Providence will return to pull you out of any difficulty as a story I once heard suggests:

A guy is walking down the street when he falls into a hole. The hole is so deep he can't get out.

A doctor passes by, and the guy shouts up, "Hey you can you help me out?"

The Doctor writes a prescription, throws it down the hole, and moves on.

Then a priest passes the hole, and the guy shouts up, "Hey Father, I'm down this hole can you help me out?"

The priest writes out a prayer, throws it down the hole, and moves on.

And then a friend walks by, and the guy shouts up, "Hey buddy can you help me out?"

The friend jumps in the hole, and the guy says, "Are you stupid? Now we are both down here!"

"Yeah but I've been down here before," the friend says, "and I know the way out."

As the story reveals, the help you require often comes in the form of someone who *knows* the Way out. This person will often have succeeded in the Way that you too hope to succeed, or he or she will embody a quality that you most definitely need if you are to realise your potential and fulfil your ambitions.

The one who knows the Way will frequently come into your life at the most opportune time when your need is at its greatest. As the Buddhist proverb goes, "When the student is ready the teacher appears."

Having been humbled by the scale of the challenge before you, or unsettled by the great uncertainty you face, you will now be most ready and willing to learn all that this mentor or friend will have to teach you.

When this teacher does make an appearance in your life, it may surprise you just how much he or she will be willing to give you of their time and wisdom. There is a *good* reason for this. They too will have followed their heart to pursue some great purpose that mattered to them. They, like you, will also have found themselves embroiled in a desperate struggle at some critical point along the Way. They too will have received the help they now offer to you with such an open heart.

When the student is ready the teacher appears. The one who knows the Way will come your Way.

They will gladly 'jump in the hole' with you and stand where you stand in life for they will have no fear of losing their Way.

They will know how to uplift you and get you on your Way again.

If you have not found the teacher you need, have faith that he or she will come. Remember, also that life can teach us in many ways. For now, I hope that this book will serve you well as your guide; for it is written from the heart and it shares with you the wisdom that was handed to me when I most needed it.

If today you were to come across someone who knows the Way, he or she would no doubt tell you that the Way out of any deep hole, difficulty or crisis is this:

You must decide who you are going to be at this time in your life.

I believe this is one of the greatest choices we can make. This free will to decide who you choose to be in any situation is one the most valuable gifts that life grants us all.

Unfortunately many fail to see or make use of this gift when it would be most beneficial to do so. When a testing situation reveals some character flaw, many feel powerless to do anything about it. Believing that they cannot change, they hypnotise themselves with this limiting thought. They shackle their minds, constrain their hearts, and fail to make use of the power that lies dormant within them to be something greater than they may have been in the past.

If you are being held back in life, for whatever reason, from being who you want to be, you must take hold of the *story* being played out in your own heart and mind. If you are serious about transforming yourself, that is.

This story is what you *believe* your life is about; specifically what you *believe* has happened in the past, what you *believe* is happening to you now, and what you *believe* can happen in the future.

You are the central character in the story. Only you can decide who you are going to be, in relation to the big turning points in your life. Knowing that what you believe is possible will write the script and determine how your story will play out.

If you believe you are powerless to change who you are, your life story remains *fixed* and uninspired. By acting out who you have always been, the power of habit forces you to move through life by compulsion rather than choice. If you find yourself unable to change and adapt to life's many challenges, there is a great danger that fear and not hope will dominate your future thinking.

If on the other hand, you believe that something greater lies within you and that *you have the power to change*, your life will become more expansive, and you will discover a growing ability to *freely* express who you really want to be at any given moment of your life.

By living this Way, you will realise that every crisis is really an opportunity to *define who you are.* The periods of difficulty you face may for a time expose your weaknesses, but they will also give you the perfect opportunity to build your character. *This is the real blessing of any crisis.*

Decide who you are going to be in the big moments of your life, when the Way tests you the most.

In fact, whether it is a crisis or opportunity that now lies before you, know that there is real power in deciding who you choose to be. No matter how hard you are pushed by testing circumstances or no matter how great the opportunity that is presented to you, you will discover that *a greater power resides within you* that is always ready to assist when you make the empowering decision to do (or be) something that your heart believes is a good thing.

Given that having faith in a greater power within you is the golden thread that runs through every page of this book, let me share a personal experience that has shaped my own story:

One day, a strange thought came to me.

"What would it be like to forget everything?" it asked.

The question immediately captivated my mind which began churning over and over again with this same intriguing thought.

"What would it be like to forget everything? What would it be like to forget everything..? What would it be like to forget everything?"

For what seemed like hours, this thought began to spin faster and faster in my mind like a relentless vortex.

"What would it be like to forget everything..? What would it be like to forget everything..? What would it be like to forget everything?" it repeatedly asked.

As I wondered if this thought would ever stop, all of a sudden everything became still and silent.

In that stillness, a Voice spoke within me.

"The power of negativity works by sowing the seeds of doubt in your mind," it said with conviction.

Next, I experienced a powerful surge of energy flow through me that felt incredibly blissful. In the rush and exhilaration of the experience, I felt as though I had momentarily let go of everything that had ever held me back and that I could be anything I willed myself to be.

At that moment I sensed beyond doubt that the power
within me was free, unlimited, and beyond measure.

As ineffable as this experience was, I *intuitively* knew I had received a glimpse of something greater within me – an infinite power that I believe resides in us all; a tremendous force for good that is always ready to serve our best interests and respond to our best intentions; a 'feel good' energy that can empower you to become all you desire to be.

It is only when we doubt ourselves, and the power within us, that we limit our potential to become the person in our heart of hearts we would most like to be.

A greater power resides within you. It will
empower you to become what
you really desire.

It is vitally important therefore that you *believe in the power within you* if you want to succeed in your aims and thrive in your life. If you can maintain this belief, *no matter what*, you will discover how truly capable you are when you have to dig deep in life and find something more within yourself.

As I suggested before, it does not matter what you believe this power to be. Whether you believe it is spiritual, mental, emotional, or physical in origin is immaterial. What is important is that you make conscious use of this great power to transform yourself and your world for the better.

Start now by deciding who you are going to be from this moment onward in your life.

Ask yourself, what quality must you build into your character to take your journey to the next level?

Do you need to be courageous and decisive or are calmness and patience required to make the difference? Will creativity, passion, or skill open up the Way? Or does life now require you to be humble and willing to learn if you are going to master what it takes to get ahead?

There may, however, be a more pressing question on your mind. You might be asking, how exactly can you be something that you have never been before?

The answer is that you must *act the part* until you become the part. You must *act as if* you already possess the quality you need and believe that it is within you. You must *imagine your ideal self* and make every effort to be that person to the greatest possible degree today.

However, be under no illusion. This Work will be difficult. It will feel unnatural and awkward at first to be something you have never been before. As all of us discover (sooner or later), old habits and behaviours die hard and will be resistant to change.

**To become what you desire, act the part
until you become the part.**

But you must have the conviction to press on regardless. As every new challenge or crisis presents itself, be determined to stay true to your ideal self and make every effort to be who you want to be.

Be prepared, however, to stand up for who you want to be, and what you want to do. Do not let your doubts, fears, and inhibitions get in your Way. Do not let an old inferior 'way of being' re-assert itself over what you now believe is a more desirable Way to be.

More now than ever you must *believe in your power to become something more*; to become who you most desire.

Brace yourself. The Work will require great commitment if you want to go further. Know that you will need to earn the right to get ahead. You will need to have the *ongoing courage* to step up and be what is required when the big moments of destiny come your Way. *This is the Way you will thrive.*

The future you desire very much depends on who you decide to be right now.

CHAPTER 5

Earn the right to get ahead

A great teacher once said, "I tell you the truth, unless you change and become like little children, you will never enter the kingdom of heaven."

We could define heaven as a place in which we can become everything we desire to be. We could say therefore that this heaven we seek is within us – it is the greater state of mind we enter when we *imagine* and *believe* that we can become the ideal person we long to be and that we can create the ideal life we desire.

We freely entered this heaven when we were little children, and we resided in the blissful state of make-believe. In the happiest moments of our childhood, we used everything at our disposal to escape into realms of fantasy in which we played out great adventures with our siblings and friends.

When playing 'let's pretend' we imagined becoming our favourite heroes. We did our best to move like they moved, to talk like they talked, and to do whatever great things we imagined they did.

Unfortunately, however, many people lose touch with this heaven as the years roll on. Many of us get caught up in everyday pressures or mundane concerns that leave little time for creative or imaginative Work. As many of us encounter failure, disappointments, and moments of crisis, we stop thinking about what might be and we starve our dreams of the belief they need to grow.

Perhaps most disappointingly, many of us forget about our heroes and many of us fall short of the person we once hoped, or desired, we would become when we were 'older'.

There comes a time, however, when the 'heaven within' calls out to you again. Through your heart and intuition, it reminds you of the power within you to *imagine and make real what you believe is possible.*

As children we played make-believe. The time now is to make real what you believe is possible.

It seeks to inspire you with a thought that has been voiced by many courageous souls of all backgrounds and faiths who have dared to follow their hearts and fulfil their potential. That inspiring thought is:

"Everything is possible for the one who believes."

We did believe everything was possible when we played the childhood game of make-believe. Back then, we were not held back by inhibitions or limiting thoughts. Being 'free spirits,' we were naturally good at 'acting the part' that our imaginations asked us to play.

The grown up game of *'make real what you believe is possible'* presents a much greater level of challenge that will test your talent, faith, and character. If you hope to emulate or even surpass the achievements of your heroes and idols, know that *you will need to earn the right to get ahead.* To make real what you believe is possible, you now have to act the part *until* you become the part; becoming the part is no easy thing to do. This Work requires tremendous *time,* e*ffort,* and above all else, *belief.*

The belief – that you have the power to manifest what your heart desires and to become who you most aspire to be – must be strong enough to stand the test of time. It must also be strong enough to propel you beyond any doubts, fears, and failures that hold you back; especially when the *big moments of destiny* come calling your Way which challenge you to become more than you have ever been in the past.

This is the formidable and thrilling Work that the Way now demands:

To fulfil your potential, you will need to be humble enough to believe in a power greater than yourself.

Whatever you call this 'power' — Life, Providence, God, Destiny, Kismet, Fate or something more personal like your Heart, Soul, or Intuition – you will need to *put your complete trust in it* and have faith that it will always help you find the Way to go. To access its full potential, you will need to do what you naturally did as a child – *believe once more in the magic of life.*

Believe in the magic of life.
Believe a greater power guides your Way.

To show you how, let's go back to the story that began this book. It reveals the remarkable sequence of events that helped me find my own Way but more importantly it demonstrates everything that this book is about.

In telling you this story, it is not my wish to draw attention to myself; only to the *magical and life-affirming* path that is revealed by following your heart and intuition. Know that I don't use the word 'magic' lightly when describing either life or this process. I refer instead to one of the primary definitions of the word which is 'the power of apparently influencing events by a supernatural or metaphysical force.' Keep this magic in mind as you read the story that follows:

Eight years ago, I was handed a newspaper article by a friend who I was meeting for coffee. It featured the story of a man who had started life as a taxi driver but who had – through a remarkable career – become the personal manager and close friend to one of the world's most recognised and influential sporting celebrities.

He then said something that surprised me.

"You need to meet this guy!" he told me excitedly.

"Why and how would we ever meet?" I replied.

"I don't know. I just get the feeling you need to meet this guy," he replied in all seriousness.

Without giving it too much thought, I moved the conversation on. The idea seemed a little farfetched. At the time the man in question lived in another country and worked in another world entirely to the conventional world of banking in which I found myself at the time. It seemed crazy to entertain any notion that the two of us would ever meet. But here's the craziest part of it all, four years later we did meet and over time it became increasingly apparent that we needed to meet.

So what brought us together?

I could go as far back as my childhood in recounting the intricate sequence of events that led to that meeting. Let's start, however, when I was 24… 12 years before I met the man in question.

At the time I was working for a big global firm, but my heart was not in the job. I felt like I wanted to **be something more**; *I wanted to do something that helped and inspired others, but I only had* **a vague idea** *of what that was and I had no clue as to how I could earn a living doing it.*

A moment of opportunity, however, came my Way. *The firm where I worked was taken over and was offering voluntary redundancies in a bid to cut costs. I still remember the words of my boss when I told him I wanted to take up this option.*

"We don't want you to leave, Jag," he said, "and I would caution you against doing anything too precipitous."

That word – precipitous –stood out in my mind. It means 'anything done suddenly without careful consideration.' The idea in mind might have been vague but I believed it was the Way to go, so **I followed my heart,** *decided to* **be more adventurous**, *and I pushed for redundancy.*

As soon as I got the financial payoff, I invested in something my heart led me to believe was the right thing — a course to become a performance coach who could help others realise their potential.

I spent the next 12 months gaining the qualification I needed, only for the fear of going it alone to get the better of me when I was about to embark on this change in career. Something within me told me I wasn't ready yet.

*I suddenly felt I had lost my Way. I had no idea in which direction to go. However, **a mentor came my Way at just the right time** who gave me the clarity I required at that moment. She suggested that I needed to **be patient** for I had first to prove I could make my own Way in life before I could help anyone else do the same.*

*She also said, "**Seek silence often** and use that quiet time to **listen to your heart** and to **visualise the opportunity you desire**. The right doors will keep opening up, and right opportunities will keep coming your Way if you do."*

*So at the same time, every day, I **faithfully** did just that. I imagined attracting the perfect opportunity that would allow me to find my Way.*

Months later, I was driving past a building that I drove past most days of the week; it was the office of one of the big UK banks. I had never taken any special notice of it before, except this time I got an **intuitive feeling** *about something. I turned to my wife, who was in the car with me and I pointed to the building and said, "I've got this strange feeling I'm going to work there."*

She looked back at me as though I was crazy but the feeling persisted.

A few weeks later, I was on a train to London going to a job interview for another company, when the train came to a standstill. The conductor announced there was some delay ahead that would stop the train from moving for 30 minutes or so. At that moment, the woman who was sat opposite me took a folder out of her bag which had the same company logo of the Bank where I had the feeling I was going to work. Immediately I sensed it was **a sign**, *and I struck up a conversation with her. I didn't tell her about my crazy hunch, but I did about the fact that I needed a job.*

The one-hour conversation that followed literally changed the course of my life. It turned out she worked at the building I had pointed out to my wife. At the end of the train journey, she turned to me and said, "You would love working for the bank and especially for my boss."

She then insisted that I should meet him. Weeks later I did, and he offered me a job. I spent the next nine years of my life working at that bank because of that one train conversation!

At almost the same time that I started working there, I had the spontaneous experience I described in the last chapter where I was given a glimpse of the power within and the blissful 'realisation' that I could be anything I willed myself to be.

As the years rolled on, that experience never left me, nor the feeling that one day I would leave the bank to do the Work that really mattered to me: to inspire others to become who they wanted to be.

I had no idea when, or how, that would happen but at the time I was about 29, I had a memorable talk with another mentor of mine about how much I wanted to leave the bank. During that conversation he said something that stuck with me.

"If you're still at the bank by the time your 35, you're screwed!" he said in no uncertain terms, "If that happens you'll be there for life."

*His words created the desired effect. Immediately, I decided that I needed to **be more determined to find the Way**. I began by coaching my friends for free* *outside of my day job in order to sharpen the skills that I believed would later be called upon.*

I also decided it was time to **be more creative** *and to* **be more committed** *by completing the latest fictional story that I was writing; I hoped that it would inspire others. I should tell you that writing a book was something else that I felt, in my heart, that I wanted to do (since I was 25). I had written two stories in the past and sent them to a number of publishers, only for both to be rejected.*

After a short burst of excitable effort, I completed the manuscript and sent it off to some publishers, only for it to be rejected with the same generic reasons I had received in response to my earlier efforts – the book wasn't quite right, or it didn't quite fit with the publisher's list.

At that moment, full of anger and frustration, I vowed never to write anything again. I also began to doubt if I would ever find my Way out of the bank. I had become good at coaching, but I wondered if it was enough to pay a mortgage and raise the family that my wife and I deeply desired.

Feeling a little distressed, I began seeking the silence and my inner guidance once again. I asked life to show me the Way. The next two years, however, were a difficult time.

I desperately wanted to leave the bank but no clear Way out emerged. Another testing challenge also presented itself as my wife and I were to struggle for years to conceive the child we both wanted more than anything else.

However, **when I needed it most, a teacher came my Way** *who represented everything I aspired to become. Meeting him was* **the inspiration and the godsend that I needed.** *It changed everything.*

He showed me that I was still some Way off where I needed to be if I truly wanted to **be of greater service to life.** *I was deeply humbled by what I had yet to learn, but it did not discourage me in any way for I now knew what was required to become who I most desired. He also advised me to* **be more open** *as to how the Way ahead would be revealed and to* **believe in the magic of life once more.**

Soon after (and not long before I was handed the newspaper article of the man I mentioned at the start of this story) I began to have a recurring dream that I was working in and around professional footballers. At first, I thought it was because I had come close to making it as a footballer in my early twenties and that it was some unfulfilled dream that was playing out in my mind.

However, I sensed it was something more than that as it **sparked off my passion** *for football once again. Taking a greater interest in it, I started seeing more in the sport; especially how each player expressed who he was by how he played the game. Inspired by what I saw, short poetic verses began coming to me about how we could play any game better – especially the 'game of life.'.*

Soon I had 101 of these verses which I **speculatively** *sent off to a publisher. To my surprise they expressed a desire in helping me to publish this piece of work which was the shortest thing I had ever written; and at the age of 34, whilst still working for the bank, I became the author of a little book called* **'Playing the Beautiful Game.'**

Publishing the book was the slice of **'beginner's luck'** *I needed. It was the first significant win that set me on my Way. It gave me the faith and courage needed to* **take a big leap of faith***, when the opportunity came my Way to reach a financial settlement with the bank that would allow me to leave at the age of 35.*

Just after leaving, I was approached by another part of the bank, who asked if I could host a two-day event for them. I told them I wasn't really a presenter, and I was about to decline the opportunity when my intuition told me to **be more open and do it!**

On the first night of the event, I met a larger-than-life venture capitalist who insisted late that evening that I should go out with him and few others on a big night out. I declined, but he persisted. He said, "I'm going to get my coat. By the time I come back let me know what you've decided…but whatever happens, you're coming!"

*I had a good reason to say no. I was presenting early in the morning again, and it was already past midnight. But my intuition told me to **be more daring and go!***

I'm glad I did. The man who insisted I go became one of my clients and, six months later, he asked if I had a spare copy of 'Playing the Beautiful Game.' He told me he wanted to give it to a man whose company he had just invested in. He said, "I get this feeling that you two will really get on. This guy has managed two of the biggest footballers on the planet. I think your book is right up his street!"

*I was completely blown away when he revealed who the man in question was; it was none other than the man featured in the article that my friend had given me four years earlier (who, at the time, my friend suggested I really needed to meet). I was amazed that **life had contrived a Way to make it happen**.*

When the two of us did meet, it became clear within minutes that we would really get on.

At just the right time, Providence had brought us together for a good reason. *We were to become a part of each other's Work of inspiring talented individuals to fulfil their potential; we were to provide valuable support to each other at a critical stage in our careers; but more than that we were to become friends and fellow adventurers on the Way.*

All the events of this story are true. There are, however, hundreds of other meaningful coincidences and unexpected and favourable situations that came my Way that I haven't mentioned that are equally a part of the story. If I were to narrate all the intricate events in detail, they would easily fill the pages of a book many times this size.

My intention, however, is to share just enough of the story in order to reveal the *'pattern of events'* that I have seen play out many times when a firm decision is made to follow the heart.

Through pursuing the Way, and helping others to do the same, I have formed a deep respect for the awe-inspiring Way in which Providence – *the magic of life* – is able to make things happen when you put your complete belief and trust in it.

The sure fire Way in which the journey of the heart unfolds leads me to believe, without any doubt, that there is a greater intelligence at work behind the scenes that has a plan, that knows what it's doing, and that has all the required 'magic' to make it happen.

> **Have the courage to act on your dream.**
> **Unexpected and favourable situations will**
> **come your Way.**

If you are able to believe in the magic of life, it can help you step up at any moment and be something more; something that will make all the difference in how your life will unfold. Know that the future you desire is therefore at stake *right now*. As Shakespeare intimated in his immortal line from Hamlet, *"To be or not to be, that is the question."*

The decision to consciously be whatever this moment requires, and to act the part until you become the part, will be a life and career-defining choice. The decision you make will ripple out ahead of you and change your future years from now in an almost inconceivable Way.

If you can, in this very minute, commit to being the person you know in your heart you can be, you can start making the kind of waves that will later come back to you laden with the success and fulfilment you most desire.

The decision to be more daring, open, and adventurous at this point in your life may initiate your own unforeseen and inspiring chain of events that can connect you in due course with the right people and right opportunities upon which your desired future will be built.

Everything will depend on what you choose to do, who you choose to be, and what you choose to believe is possible.

Do not move on from this last sentence until its profound importance has sunk into your mind and reverberated in your heart.

Step up and be more daring in this moment.
Your decision will ripple out and shape the
future you desire.

The more you make every attempt to be the man or woman you want to be, the more you will begin to realise that you *do* possess the power within you to transform yourself and your future in the Way you desire.

The more you can *act the part* you want to play in life, the stronger and more positive the ripple will be that you send out into your future, and the greater your power will grow to attract everything you need to *become the part*.

This is how to *master your destiny* and to become who you most desire. This is how to go deeper into the Work of turning your inspiration into application. When you have truly found your calling, and you have made progress along the Way, your heart will then entice you forward with a compelling new thought:

Imagine how good you can be if you really Worked your talent.

This 'best version' of yourself will be the perfect expression of your talent that you believe is possible; becoming it will turn into a never-ending quest; the further you go, the more you'll continue to find within yourself.

If you can Work your talent, and strive for perfection, a great reward lies in wait; for you will experience sublime moments in life where everything comes together, and you are taken *beyond* what you believe is possible. Then, *you will thrive* more than even your greatest expectations.

CHAPTER 6

Master the Way to express yourself

As short as this book is, the journey it seeks to bring to life may span a whole lifetime. If you faithfully follow your heart, find the Work you love and make every attempt to be who you want to be, a time will come when the Way before you will open out to greater possibilities.

When you prove to yourself that you possess the magic to make things happen, the magnetism to attract all that you require to succeed, and the power to make good your aims, you will earn great freedom to live life your Way.

No-one or nothing will have the power to hold you back for you will realise that the power within you is immense. By successfully following your own path in life, you will no longer care too much about other people's opinions of you, nor worry too much about impressing anybody else.

Nothing or no-one can hold you back
when you realise the power you
possess is immense.

Doing what *you* value, and being what *inherently* feels good, you will discover that you are not beholden to anyone nor imprisoned by what other people think of you. You will no longer need any form of external approval as to who you should be or what you should do. Instead, you will enjoy the great freedom of expression that flows when you simply *let go and be who in your heart of hearts you really want to be.* If you earn the right to be free in this Way, everything you experience will prepare you for a time in your life when you are ready to reach up and *find the ideal opportunity* that will make the very most of your talent; this will be the perfect stage upon which to *express yourself to the greatest possible extent.*

The success and failures you experience along the Way will *galvanise* your character in readiness. The moments of crisis you overcome will give you the *fearlessness* you need. The moments of exhilaration you taste will give rise to an *unquenchable thirst to go further* that can help you reach the most exalted peak of success you can imagine.

The Way to get ahead may have started with a vague idea of what you wanted to do, and who you wanted to become, but with every hard-earned victory and with every inch of progress you make along the Way, the idea of success you have in mind will become bigger, bolder, and more definite. The difference you feel you can make in life will become equally more clear and compelling.

If others come to know of how glorious and well-defined your dream has become, they may believe it's too audacious even to attempt. However, with every leap of faith you take and every big moment of destiny you grasp, you will build the inner belief and courage you'll need to conquer what others might believe are unassailable heights.

The further you go on the Way, the less deterred you will become by how far ahead the Way stretches out before you. Nor will you be fazed by the steep climb that stands between you and the highest stage that you believe you can reach. If you have made it your goal to hit these rarefied heights, you will need to *master the Way to express yourself.*

With belief, you will conquer what others believe are unassailable heights.

This Work can never be taken lightly. Be prepared to spend hours and hours of time acting the part until you become the part. Be prepared to express who you want to be *over and over again* until it becomes a definite part of who you are. It may go without saying but be clear in your mind:

The greater you hope to be, the greater the effort required to become it.

If you hope to thrive more than ever before, start now by perfecting your art, mastering your skill, and unlocking your fullest potential. Know that as you begin this arduous Work, others may not understand what is driving you to push beyond all that you have achieved already. If you have made much progress on the Way, others may ask, "Why go on any further when you've already done so much?"

The author Annie Payson Call provided a compelling answer to this question in her timeless piece of work called 'Power Through Repose' (1891):

> *An old artist who thanked his friend for admiring his pictures added: "If you could only see the pictures in my brain. But," pointing to his brain and then to the ends of his fingers, "the channels from here to here are so long!"*

Like the artist, you will have an ideal picture in your mind that your heart will want to make real. This perfect vision or dream will become so distinct, so rich, and so enticing, that you will not be able to rest until you have made every possible effort to realise it. There is a line from a song that I remember from my youth that captures the sentiment perfectly: *'If I hadn't seen such riches I could deal with being poor!'*

When you become aware of the rich possibilities that life has to offer, you will go all out to have and experience them; this is true of material riches but especially so of the greater riches of talent that lie within you.

Whatever your talent, you will want to spend your days honing it, refining it and perfecting it so that you can flawlessly express the beautiful and uplifting possibilities that take shape in your mind.

You will find great meaning in this Work, for the greater you become, the greater the possibility you represent to others of what is achievable.

The question now is what possibility would you love to represent in life?

If you can represent the fantastic possibility that by doing the Work you can achieve what your heart desires, you will inspire others to do the same. In mastering the Way, you will also light up a path for others to follow. As Gandhi said, *"Be the change you want to see in the world."* By being all that you can be, you can consciously play your part in transforming the world into a more extraordinary place.

When greater possibilities begin taking shape in your mind, your heart will go all out to experience them for real.

If you're ready to master the Way to express yourself:

Be observant so that you may learn from those who lead the Way. Train your eye to notice the differences in skill – and richness of talent – that separate the best from the chasing pack.

Be humble so that you may also learn from those who are just a hair's breadth in front of you, for they too may represent a possibility that you are yet to master.

Be secure if the Work requires you to compete with others to get ahead on the Way. Respect your rivals but acknowledge that the only person you are ever really competing with is the best-imagined version of yourself.

Be committed for you cannot afford to dissipate your energy, waste any time, nor miss any opportunity that comes your Way to refine your talent. One lifetime will never feel like it's enough to truly master the Way.

Be patient for you may have to go backwards in order to keep going forward. You may need to re-master the basics of your profession to ensure that any bad habits you have acquired along the Way do not later compromise and constrain your talent.

Be determined in order to keep reinventing yourself. Mastering the next level of skill, the next best move, or the next rung on the ladder will become a never-ending process of refinement.

Be focused so that you never lose sight of the greater power within you to always go beyond what you believe are the limits of your potential.

Work your talent to master the Way.

Do not underestimate, however, the prodigious amount of Work that is required to master the Way and close in on the best version of yourself – the most perfect expression of your talent – that you can imagine.

Do not underestimate how much of this Work will need to be done away from the world – in your own time – without anyone to pat you on the back or commend you for your effort.

When your date with destiny does finally come your Way, and you experience what at the time feels like your crowning glory of success, you may cry tears of joy *and* pain; for only you will know everything you have sacrificed and everything you have given to have come so far.

For many, striving for this level of perfection is too heavy a price to pay. For many the toll of pursuing their best becomes too much; mastering their craft simply becomes too difficult. This is the reason why great talent is always in big demand but in short supply; it is why sizeable rewards lie in wait for those who arrive at the top; and why these rewards flow more freely for those who show promise of reaching this summit.

If your heart is in your Work, however, your desire to master the Way to express yourself will become a labour of love and the rewards you will earn will go far beyond the external gains of wealth and worldly recognition.

The gift of *effortless mastery* is one such prize. Through doing the Work, you will come to realise that any skill which takes great effort to master can, in time, be powerfully and freely expressed with (what will seem to others) minimal effort.

Effortless mastery is one of nature's great blessings. To appreciate this gift, you need only see how a small child masters (through great effort) how to walk – falling, failing, and stumbling along the Way – before her world opens out with wonderful possibilities and she learns how to playfully make her Way through life with ever greater levels of freedom and ease.

It is this same natural ability that will free your own potential to thrive in life. With every new talent you master, you will unlock a greater capability within you to learn something new, to master something else and to become something more. This is one of the cornerstones of all success:

For those who continue to do the Work more is always possible.

Through greater Work, another considerable reward is earned along the Way – *unshakeable poise*. With poise, you will be able to express yourself effortlessly and masterfully but above all else *fearlessly* when it really matters. With poise, you will be able to reproduce your magic over and over again when life really demands it. With poise, you will be able to stand up and deliver when the world looks on with great expectation.

True poise can only be attained when you are able to transform belief into courage and courage into *confidence*. This cycle forever proceeds along the same line. When you first imagine what you might be able to achieve with belief, you will say, *"I think I can."* When you take a leap of faith towards the realisation of your goal with courage, you will say, *"I will see if I can."* When you have mastered what the Way requires, with *confidence*, you will be able to say *"I know I can!"*

As we have said, every *definite* decision to be something more, and every effort you make to act the part until you become the part, invokes the magic of life into operation. All the right doors will keep opening. All the right people will keep coming your Way. All the right opportunities will 'magically' line up and lead you to the perfect opportunity to *express yourself to the greatest possible extent.*

When you do finally arrive on this most befitting stage to showcase your talent, it is the poise you have cultivated along the Way that will allow you to *let go and be in the moment.* It is the trust in the Work you have done that will allow you to *open up and express yourself.* With great freedom and unbridled joy, you will then be able to *express who you are through what you do,* and you will realise that it's not what you do in life that ultimately defines you: it's *the Way* you do your Work that does. Martin Luther King captured the spirit of this perfectly when he said, "If it falls your lot to be a street sweeper, go out and sweep streets like Michelangelo painted pictures, sweep streets like Handel and Beethoven composed music, sweep streets like Shakespeare wrote poetry. Sweep streets so well that all the hosts of heaven and earth will have to pause and say: here lived a great street sweeper who swept his job well."

> **It's not what you do in life that defines you. It's the Way you do your Work that does.**

It is only when you are secure in the knowledge that you possess all the skill you need that you can truly cut loose and express yourself. It is only when you no longer have to think too hard about what it is that you do, that you can then enjoy the thrill of being who you want to be. It is then that your talent will shine most brightly in life. It is then that you will *really* thrive.

Think for a moment of what talent you possess. Imagine how you could transform it by *being* more bold, daring, and dynamic. Imagine how perfectly you could express it by *being* more composed, calm, and creative.

As with every step along the Way, it's who you *choose* to be when you do what you do that makes the telling difference. It is this *'being in the doing'* that heightens your self-expression. It is the *Way* you go about your Work that transforms your inspiration into application.

Expressed another way, it is the *spirit* in which you do something that elevates your Work, no matter what that Work is. It is the spirit in which you do something that uplifts you on the Way. It is for this reason why I believe *the Work and the Way is 'spiritual' at heart*.

Whenever you *express yourself with greater spirit*, you become more inspired and who you are connects more deeply with what you do. On occasions, you may even experience the majestic feeling of *being completely at one with what you're doing*. In these rare and special moments you receive a beautiful glimpse of the great depth of potential within you as your body and mind is elevated into a *'super-conscious state'* or what we can simply call the *'S-State'*.

When you express yourself with greater spirit, you will unlock a higher dimension of possibility on the Way.

Expressing yourself in the S-State is one of the greatest rewards on the Way. Spontaneously, you find yourself rising into a higher dimension of possibility. As you surpass yourself and effortlessly perform *beyond* your best, everything you have struggled so valiantly to master in the past comes together perfectly and exceeds your expectations.

With greater rhythm than you have ever known, every move you make is perfectly timed and perfectly executed as you experience the liberation of expressing yourself without fear or any thought of failure.

Paradoxically, the brilliance of the S-State unfolds without any thought or effort on your part. In these awe-inspiring moments – your mind becomes silent – and the greater power within you takes the reins and propels you past the limits of what you believe is possible.

When you emerge from the S-State, the great possibilities you have glimpsed will redefine your thinking. You will now want to set your sights even higher and aim for the greater level of perfection you have briefly touched. You will feel compelled to reproduce its magic. You will be prepared to do whatever Work it takes to lift and hold yourself at this greater level that you now know lies within you.

Like the devoted artist who makes it his Work to paint the picture that surpasses the beauty of anything he has created in the past, you too will desire nothing more than to express the greater possibilities that now captivate your own mind.

With these greater possibilities in mind, know that your heart is standing by, ready to take you on a greater adventure – no matter how far you have already come on the Way. The desire and belief that is pulsing within you is rippling out powerfully and shaping your future possibilities as we speak.

If you are wondering how far you can still go, know that the *magic of life* will never fail to amaze you. Just when you think you have seen it all, it will conjure up a bigger and better possibility for you to reach out and grasp.

**No matter how far you have already come
on the Way, your heart is standing by to
reveal what more you can become.**

In time – *as you magnetically attract all the good that comes your Way* – what may seem to others as an unbelievable journey of serendipity, chance or luck, you will know *without a doubt* is the Work of Providence.

These are the magnificent rewards for you to claim when you make the inspiring decision to follow your heart, to do the Work and to go all the Way to becoming everything you desire.

Every challenge you face, every crisis you overcome, and every move you make along the Way that requires great faith on your part will only make these rewards all the sweeter and more deserved, when the magic of life does finally bring them your Way.

As I leave you now to pursue your dream, always remember:

Life will test you, Providence will guide you, and your heart will always reveal the Way to thrive.

Remember the Way

'You Will Thrive' reveals the Way to personal fulfilment that grants you the perfect opportunity to make a telling difference and a richer contribution to life. In writing this humble guide, I have purposely intended to keep the book as short as possible; for I believe it is the brevity and simplicity of its message that makes it valuable in an age when so many people are struggling to find the time to read a book from cover to cover.

I hope, given its size, you will return to this book many times (when it most benefits you to do so) to re-read the words of guidance it has to offer and the wisdom it contains which has been revealed to me by a number of great teachers whom I have had the privilege, and good fortune, of meeting on the Way.

I believe that with each meaningful step forward you take in your own life, you will discover more in the pages of this book with every subsequent reading you make; for I have no doubt that the more you bring to it (in terms of experience, faith, and desire) the more you will stand to gain from it and the more *you will thrive* on the Way.

The central message of this book can be simply stated:

There is a great power that resides within you that can help you to become all that you desire to be.

As this book has endeavoured to show you, you can invoke this power by following your heart and pursuing the Way to thrive in life that matters the most to you.

As simple as these words are to write, they are not always easy to remember. In the relentless comings and goings of life, we can understandably and quite easily lose our Way. In times of overexcitement, we can literally get carried away. At times in which we become overly despondent, we can lose the heart and courage needed to pursue the Way. Alternatively, in those frustrating moments – when we see no immediate reward for our effort – we can lose faith in the Way.

In any such moments, where the events of your life threaten to overwhelm you, or lead you astray from what you believe and know is important in your heart, it will serve you to *remember the Way.*

To help you in the most testing of times (when you may not have the time to read this book in its entirety) read and re-read the summary points that follow in the pages ahead. They will remind you of the life-affirming Way to thrive in life. When needed, they will uplift you into an altogether more inspiring place and connect you to wisdom, power, and intelligence that resides in your heart and which is so wonderfully revealed by your intuition.

Seek the Way ahead that matters

Search deep within yourself for your heartfelt motivation – *your inner spark*. It is revealed by knowing exactly who you want to be and exactly what you want to do in life.

If you have you have lost your spark and lost your Way, seek a direction that has more *meaning* in life – *a greater purpose or calling that will inspire your mind and appeal to your heart.*

To find your *calling*, do something that *matters* in the world. To thrive, turn your thoughts from having the best, and being the best, to the rewarding purpose of *giving your best*.

Your *calling* is the Way to get ahead that stirs your heart into action. It is the Work that gives you the perfect platform to use your talent to thrive in life.

The Way *demands* that you do *the Work* required to turn your heartfelt dream into a glorious reality. Remember, this Work is the ability to *turn your inspiration into application*.

Listen to your heart and your *intuition* will speak to you. It *knows* the Way to get ahead. It can give you all the answers you need. To follow your heart, you must trust your intuition – the greater power that resides within you.

Set aside time to become *still* and *calm* to hear the voice of your intuition. If you can relax your body and quieten your mind, you will discover that it will give you a firm thought or feeling of what you need to do and the Way you need to go.

Remember that your heart and intuition will not tell you to do or become something selfish or reckless. If you trust them, they will always lead you to the greatest possible good for all concerned in each and every situation you face.

Be open to how your intuition will give you the *inspirational idea* you need to spark the Way into life. You may only dimly sense this idea at first. However, if you follow your heart and pursue your passion, the Way to thrive in life will unfold from right where you are.

Do what you love to open up the Way

Remember the Way is not one of forced obligation that wears you down and kills your spirit. *It is an opportunity* to live a fuller and more meaningful life. It is the chance to become something or someone who adds greatly to the world.

Only you can know the direction to take in life that will most excite your heart. Find the best Way to use your talent to do something you care about; to do something rewarding; to do something that you *love*.

Do what you love and you will give your best without reservation. It is the passion for your Work that compels you always to break new ground and make the most of your unique talents and gifts.

When your passion compels you to give life your all, it then becomes your *ruling passion*. It is then that all other 'lesser' and competing interests will fall away and give you the time and space to perfect your talent.

To go forward with your passion, you must first *go within*. Venture forth into your imagination and *picture what you would most love to do in life*. This is the *ideal* that you want to pursue, the dream you want to chase, and the vision you want to make real.

Set aside the time each day to imagine what you would love to see happen in your future. See it as best you can. *Love* this dream as though it was all unfolding right now in your life.

Remember *love is the power of attraction*. By some powerful and invisible means, this force of nature attracts everything it needs to create what it desires. It has the power to *orchestrate* events and create all the right circumstances you need to succeed in life.

When you pursue your heartfelt dream and *take a leap of faith*, 'Providence' contrives a Way to make it happen. The right people, the right circumstances, and right opportunities will converge on your path *just* when they are needed.

Look out for the nudges from your intuition and the small slices of beginner's luck that will tip the balance of your mindset in a positive direction. These nudges will give you the hope you need to *succeed in realising your dream* – if you can commit to it with all your heart.

Keep the faith when life tests you

Your *belief* in what you do will grow with every inch of progress you make on the Way. You will feel more capable, free, and alive than before. Physically, emotionally, and mentally you will have more edge. Spiritually – if you are open to it – you will sense a greater power stirring within you.

When you witness your power to attract the right opportunities your Way, you will go forward in life with a newfound confidence. With great belief, you will be prepared to go where you need to go and do what needs to be done to find the better Way you seek.

Be prepared. At some point on the Way, after you have made the courageous decision to follow your heart, you will face an onslaught of negative voices and opinions from those who prefer to keep you where you are.

Be on guard. If you allow your fears to temporarily overpower the love of what you do, your thoughts will shift from success to failure, from thriving to surviving, and from an overriding feeling of belief to that of doubt. The Way become difficult when fear is in the driving seat.

There will come a time when everything that can go wrong *does* go wrong, and you find yourself caught up in a *crisis* when you least need it. In such turbulent times, every ounce of belief you have built up along the Way will be severely tested, as will your desire to continue to follow your heart.

When you face your darkest hour, and there appears to be no Way forward, *find the faith to go on. Hold onto the one positive thought you are able to believe in* and build your faith from there.

To hand over the reins of destiny from the worrier in you (that expects the worst) to the warrior within you who will fight for what is best, you must remember one golden rule: *Think about the things you want to think about, not the things you don't.*

When your mind is plagued by doubts and fears, make an active effort to *substitute* negative thoughts that weaken you with those that are positive and uplift you. Nothing will hold you back if you can do this.

Remember that *everything happens for a reason.* Any crisis on the Way will *severely* test your character. Have faith that *life is not meant to break you but make you.* Every test of character you face will draw forth a latent quality within you that you will most definitely need along the Way.

Now decide who you are going to be

There is a blessing in every situation, no matter how difficult circumstances may be. If, when you are tested, you can see yourself without any self-deception, self-delusion, or self-pity you will know what you need to do or who you need to become to transform both yourself and your fortunes.

Remember, you are never on your own as you make your Way through life. The help you need to transform yourself will always be forthcoming when you ask for it. Providence always lies in wait ready to serve you just when you most need it.

Someone who knows the Way will frequently come into your life at the most opportune time when your need is at its greatest. Remember the Buddhist proverb: "When the student is ready the teacher appears."

The Way out of any crisis or period of difficulty is to *decide who you are going to be at this time in your life.* Every crisis is really an opportunity to *define who you are.* Testing times may reveal your weaknesses, but they will also give you the perfect opportunity to build your character.

No matter how hard you are pushed by testing circumstances or no matter how great the opportunity that is presented to you, remember *a greater power resides within you* that is always ready to assist when you make the empowering decision to become what your heart desires.

The greater power within you is a tremendous force for good that is always ready to serve your best interests and respond to your best intentions. It is only when we doubt ourselves, and the power within us, that we limit our potential to become the person in our heart of hearts we would most like to be.

It does not matter what you believe your *inner power* to be. Whether you believe it is spiritual, mental, emotional, or physical in origin is immaterial. It is more important to consciously use this great power to transform yourself and your world for the better.

To be something that you have never been before, you must *act the part* until you become the part. *Act as if* you already possess the quality you need and believe that it is within you. *Imagine the ideal self* you wish to become and make every effort to be that person to the greatest possible degree today.

Be under no illusion. Acting the part until you become the part is difficult. Old habits and behaviours will die hard. Have the conviction to press on regardless. With every new challenge or crisis you face, be determined to stay true to your ideal self and who you most want to be.

Earn the right to get ahead

The 'heaven' we seek is within us – it is the greater state of mind we enter when we *imagine* and *believe* that we can become the ideal person we aspire to be and that we can create the ideal life we desire to live.

Everything is possible for the one who believes. This is the compelling thought that has been shared by courageous souls of all backgrounds and faiths who have dared to follow their hearts and fulfil their potential.

There will always come a time in your life when your heart and intuition will seek to remind you that you possess the power within you to *imagine and make real what you believe is possible.*

Remember you will need to *earn the right to get ahead.* To make real what you believe is possible, strive valiantly in acting the part *until* you become the part. Never forget that this Work requires tremendous *time, effort*, and above all else, *belief.*

To realise your dream, you will need to believe in a power greater than yourself. Whatever you call this 'power' – Life, Providence, God, Destiny, Kismet, Fate, your Heart, Soul, or

Intuition – put your complete trust in it and believe once more in the magic of life.

Have faith that Providence – *the magic of life* – is able to make things happen when you put your complete belief and trust in it. Look out for the signs which suggest that a greater intelligence is at work behind the scenes, that has a plan, that knows what it's doing, and that has all the required 'magic' to make it happen.

Remember, the future you desire is at stake *right now*. The decision to consciously be who you want to be at this moment in your life will be a life and career-defining choice. It will ripple out ahead of you and change your desired future years from now in awe-inspiring Ways.

The more you can *act the part* you want to play in life, the stronger and more positive the ripple will be that you send out into your future, and the greater your power will grow to attract everything you need to *become the part*.

Remember, *everything in your life depends on what you choose to do, who you choose to be, and what you choose to believe is possible*. The decision to be or do something more at this very moment may initiate an unforeseen and inspiring chain of events that can connect you in due course with the right people and right opportunities upon which your desired future will be built.

Master the Way to express yourself

When you prove to yourself that you possess the magic to make things happen, the magnetism to attract all that you require to succeed, and the power to make good your aims, you will earn great freedom to live life your Way.

By doing what *you* value, and being what *inherently* feels good, you will not be beholden to anyone. Instead, you will enjoy the great freedom of expression that flows when you simply *let go and be who, in your heart of hearts, you really want to be.*

Earn the right to be who you want to be, to *find the ideal opportunity* that will make the very most of your talent. Seek this perfect stage upon which to *express yourself to the greatest possible extent.*

Courageously take every leap of faith that comes your Way. Boldly grasp the big moments of destiny that you meet and you will secure the belief you need to conquer what others believe are unassailable heights.

If you wish to hit the highest heights, *master the Way to express yourself.* Commit everything you have to perfecting your art, mastering your skill, and unlocking your fullest potential. Remember, *the greater you hope to be, the greater the effort required to become it.*

Represent the great possibility that by doing the Work, you can achieve what your heart desires. In mastering the Way, light up a path for others to follow. Be all that you can be and inspire others to do the same; and play your part in transforming the world into a more extraordinary place.

Do not dissipate your energy, waste any time, nor miss any opportunity that comes your Way to refine your skill. Commit to the Work of mastering your talent if you hope to enjoy the reward of masterfully, fearlessly, and effortlessly expressing yourself when it really matters in your life.

Know that it is the poise you have cultivated along the Way that will allow you to *let go and be in the moment*. It is the trust in the Work you have done that will allow you to *open up and express yourself*.

Remember, always, that it is the *spirit* in which you do something that elevates your Work and uplifts you on the Way. *Express yourself with greater spirit* to go beyond the limits of what you believe is possible and to thrive more than you have ever known before.

The 7 Master Moves of Success

by Jag Shoker

In this absorbing and uplifting book, Jag Shoker – a leading performance coach to business leaders, sports professionals and creative performers – brings the science and inspiration behind success to life. He reveals the *7 Master Moves* that combine to create the high performance state that he calls *Inspired Movement*: the ability to perform an optimal series of moves to create the success you desire most.

Drawing widely on scientific research, his extensive consultancy experiences, and insights into the successes of top performers in business, sport, and entertainment, *7 Master Moves* is a synthesis of the leading-edge thinking, and paradigms, that underpin personal performance and potential. Building upon key research in fields such as neuroscience, psychology, expert performance and talent development - *7 Master Moves* represents an evidence-based 'meta' theory of what really works. Compelling to read, and easy to follow, the book incorporates a strong practical element and shares a number of powerful and practical exercises that can help you apply each Master Move and achieve greater results in your life and work.

What Business Can Learn From Sport Psychology

by Dr Martin Turner & Dr Jamie Barker

The mental side of performance has always been a crucial component for success – but nowadays coaches, teams, and athletes of all levels and abilities are using sport psychology to help fulfil their potential and serve up success.

In *What Business Can Learn From Sport Psychology* readers will develop the most important weapon needed to succeed in business: their mental approach to performance. This book reveals the secrets of the winning mind by exploring the strategies and techniques used by the most successful athletes and professionals on the planet. Based on decades of scientific research, the authors' professional experiences, and the experiences of winning athletes and business professionals, this book is a practical and evidence-driven resource that will teach readers how to deal with pressure, break through adversity, embrace challenges, project business confidence, and much more.

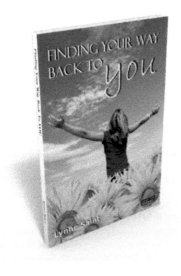

Finding Your Way Back to YOU: A self-help book for women who want to regain their Mojo and realise their dreams!

by Lynne Saint

Designed as a practical book with an accompanying downloadable journal and weblinked exercises, *Finding Your Way Back to YOU* introduces Neuro-Linguistic Programming, and Cognitive Behavioural Therapy techniques for women's change. It will help readers to develop and achieve the goals they dreamed of and show them how to increase self-confidence - removing any self-limiting beliefs that previously prevented them from getting what they want.

The author is an experienced life coach, NLP Practitioner and Hypnotherapist.

Lightning Source UK Ltd.
Milton Keynes UK
UKHW02f1022020918
328194UK00009B/383/P

9 781910 515662